About the Aut

Aloysius Yongbi Fontama is an Investor, Private Tutor, Mentor and Founder of the financial education firm of A&F Capital Advisors and A&F Tutors. A&F Tutors is an education consulting firm aimed at adding value to people through one-to-one private tutoring, mentoring, and coaching. It also uses education as a tool for social and economic mobility, especially for those from low-socioeconomic backgrounds by assisting them in acquiring financial security and freedom, by investing in the stock market.

He is also the author of two other books in line with his passion for education and investment: "How to invest in the stock market for the first time and make money" and "How to secure an apprenticeship in line with your passion and skills".

After graduating from Cass Business School City, University of London's highly prestigious Quantitative Finance and Financial Engineering course, alongside an MSc in Mathematical Trading and Finance, Mr Fontama spent a few years in various analyst roles as an Investment, Special Projects and Trading Floor Technical Analyst in Private Equity

About the Author

and Investment banking sectors. Through his experiences in investment banking, which included teaching and training other members of staff, Mr Fontama discovered his twin passions to make a positive transformation in people's lives and sharing knowledge to empower people. This is why he wrote this book – to empower people with the knowledge and skills required to help them in their journey to financial security and freedom. He has over 15 years' experience in various roles as a tutor, lecturer and analyst across education and investment banking sectors and is currently studying towards a PhD in Personal Finance Education. He also has a master's degree in Education, a BSc (Hons) in Chemistry and Chemical Processing Engineering, including Microsoft Certified Professional and Microsoft Systems Engineering Certifications (MCSE).

He wrote this book to close gaps in employment, economic and financial inequality by helping young people and adults, especially those from disadvantaged backgrounds, achieve social mobility faster through apprenticeships. This meant developing a product to educate, empower and teach them how they can secure an apprenticeship.

About the Author

Author's Journey – Excerpts from Bayes Business School Alumni Stories

Could you tell me a bit about your time at Bayes Business School?

I enrolled for the MSc in Mathematical Trading and Finance at Bayes Business School (formerly Cass) in 2006/2007 academic year, following my decision to switch to a career in Investment Banking. My time at Bayes was very challenging but rewarding. It was challenging because I had to combine a full-time job alongside a very rigorous course in Quantitative Finance and Financial Engineering. It was a combination of 3 hours of lectures twice weekly, in the evening, with coursework and 3 hours of examinations for each module, alongside workshops and training programmes such as Bloomberg Trading room sessions.

What stands out most for me was the highly quantitative nature of the course and the fact that all lecturers were experts in their field. Also, more than 80% of my classmates were already in the industry – ranging from traders, to financial engineers and quants. Hence, the environment was a perfect fit for me to acquire practical and theoretical experiences from both lecturers and classmates as someone new to the field. On reflection, after years of experience in the investment industry, I believe the course structure, content and experience at Bayes is the best for anyone preparing for a career switch or young person planning for a career in investment banking and/or financial services. It gives students the opportunity to acquire an abundance of employable skills.

How did you come to set up your own investment management company?

I was inspired by the lifestyle of my mentor who had a stock brokerage company after a successful career as an equity trader with JP Morgan. Therefore, I decided to follow a similar career path of becoming a trader and set up my own company too. But this required a career switch and the right skillset. I enrolled for the MTF programme with the hope of gaining trading skills for a career as a trader in investment banking.

About the Author

How did your course at Bayes assist you with your career to date?

My course, MSc Mathematical Trading and Finance, played a critical role in my career. I realised from employer's comments during interviews that the depth and breadth of the course is highly regarded by employers in the financial/investment banking sector. I remember the Head of Trading Floor at HSBC Asset Management saying to me during our interview over the phone that "I am very impressed with the content of your Masters training programme that is why I thought I should offer you an interview".

The knowledge gained from the programme also facilitated the process of writing up my 5-star rated investment book on Amazon – *How to invest in the stock market for the first time and make money* which has sold over 2000 copies so far, with 80 reviews to date.

About the Author

You have recently published a book which aims to teach people about the stock market, could you tell us a bit about the book and how this came about?

Firstly, with over 10 years experience of trading in the stock market since 2009, I realised learning how to invest is an essential life skill. I realised during this period that most individuals, especially from a disadvantaged backgrounds, don't have the knowledge and skillset in regard to what stocks/bonds are etc, how to invest in them, what to invest in and the best brokers to use. Therefore, due to my passion to 'level the playing field', I thought the first step was to share my experience and knowledge to educate the lay person about how they can make money in the stock market.

What has been the biggest challenge of your career so far? What has been the most rewarding part?

Most challenging part: After my studies at Bayes in 2009, I searched for a suitable job in investment banking/financial services for more than 2 years; partly due to the impact of the global crisis which hit the financial/investment industry at that time. I attended interviews at almost every investment bank within the City of London during this 2-year period.

Most Rewarding: Investing in my education for the MTF programme at Bayes Business School and continuous personal development in my areas of interest (investment and education). It has opened the doors to many opportunities, directly and indirectly, the benefits have grown exponentially since.

Do you have any advice for anyone who might want to follow in your footsteps?

Regarding career, I would say:

1. Find a career you are passionate about and aim to become the best in your field.
2. A combination of personal development, practical experience and willingness to learn would help you become the best in your field.

About the Author

3. If you have not found your passion, take up job opportunities whether it is related to your area of study/interest or not, because any job experience in life adds up and it takes you one step forward towards your goal in terms of gaining employable skills whilst earning money. Even if it is a voluntary role, take it!

4. Sometimes work experience can lead you to discover your passion and the career you would like to pursue. For example, my volunteering role for 9 months at Principal Capital Advisors laid the foundation for permanent and paid roles at Deutsche Bank and TD Securities. At TD Securities, the experience of providing IT training to other staff helped me to identify another passion of mine – teaching and training people. This laid the foundation to set up my Tutoring and education consulting business A and F Tutors. You can find out more about how to identify your passion in my apprenticeship book on Amazon – *How to secure an apprenticeship in line with your passion and skills.*

About the Author

5. Prioritise personal development by reading books and newspapers linked to your career interest and passion.
6. Work very hard, persevere in anything you are trying to achieve, be patient, "stay hungry and stay foolish".
7. No matter how challenging life or your journey towards your goal – never give up! "Sometimes the journey is more important than the destination".

For more information on private tutoring, mentoring, financial education, apprenticeship and career mentoring services, please visit our website **www.aandftutors.com** or contact us at **admin@aandftutors.com**.

We also offer financial education, financial literacy and stock market investment training programs. For more about this, please visit www.aandfcapitaladvisors.com or contact us at **aaandfcapitaladvisors@gmail.com**.

Acknowledgements

First, this book is dedicated to God the Almighty, who gave me the strength, knowledge, and wisdom to put it together. Secondly, I dedicate it to my mother Bibiana Aghigha Yongbi and late father Godfrey Chiambeng Yongbi who taught me the value of education and sacrificed all they had to ensure my siblings and I had the best education they could afford. Third, my gratitude goes to all those who have made a positive impact on my life, in particular, my late cousin, police inspector, Njua Julius whom I never had the chance to say, "thank you for your unconditional support during the most challenging period in my life."

May this book be a financial blessing in your journey to financial security in Jesus' name.

Acknowledgements

Copyright © 2020 Aloysius Yongbi Fontama

All Rights Reserved

Reproduction in whole or part without written permission from the publisher is prohibited. Parts of this book may, however, be used only in reference to support related documents or subjects.

Table of Contents

About the Author 1

Introduction 15

The Strategy Behind Addressing the Barriers to Apprenticeships 17

What is an Apprenticeship Training? 20

Why an Apprenticeship? 22

Challenges Of an Apprenticeship 25

Types Of Apprenticeship 28

What Qualification Do I Get? 32

What Does an Employer Look for In My Level 2 Apprenticeship Application? 33

Summary of the Skills required for Level 2 - Intermediate Apprenticeship 34

What comes next after completing a level 2 apprenticeship? 34

Level 3 – Advanced Apprenticeships – The equivalent of L3 BTECs at College or A-Levels 35

Table of Contents

What Will I Be Doing as An Advanced Apprentice?......36

How Is a Level 3 Apprenticeship Designed? 36

What Qualification Do I Get After an Advanced Apprenticeship Training? 37

How Do They Work? 38

Can I do An Advanced or Level 3 Apprenticeship? 39

What Kind of Apprenticeships Can You Do at Level 3?39

What Does an Employer Look for In My Application and What Skills Do I Need to Get an Advanced Apprenticeship?.40

Higher Apprenticeships (Level 4 +)..............................41

Level 4 Apprenticeships 42

Level 5 Apprenticeships 44

Requirements for Level 5 Apprenticeships 44

Level 7 Apprenticeships 45

What Are They Like?..46

What Qualification Do I Get? 46

What Kind of Apprenticeships Can You Do at A Higher Level? ...48

Table of Contents

What Does an Employer Look for In My Application?...48

Are these graduate apprenticeships? 49

How Do I Secure an Apprenticeship in Line with My Passion and Skills? 50

How I Found My Passion 54

How To Develop an Effective CV, Cover Letter and Personal Statement 60

Breakdown of What Makes a Good CV 70

Person Specification 78

How do I Prepare Effectively for My Interview? 92

Introduction

Over the years, many young people, some of whom have been our clients at A&F Tutors Ltd, and their parents have asked me several questions about apprenticeships such as:

- What are apprenticeships?

- When can they apply for apprenticeships?

- Which type of apprenticeships are suitable for them?

- Why should they apply?

- How can they go about getting an apprenticeship?

Apprenticeships are key to social, economic, and financial mobility for all young people, especially those from a disadvantaged background who need it more. In effect, apprenticeships play an essential role in addressing UK's productivity gap and future financial success because our success as a nation depends on the financial success of every individual, especially young people.

Introduction

The reason being is that **a person's family circumstances can still dictate their employment prospects.** Young people from disadvantaged families are a third more likely to drop out of education at 16 to pursue lower-skilled, lower-paid and insecure jobs; and where a child lives has a profound impact on their prospects for social mobility.

Giving young people the opportunity to learn and earn through apprenticeships is one of the best ways to bridge that gap and achieve social mobility. Therefore, the main aim of this book is to empower young people, especially those from disadvantaged backgrounds to overcome barriers to apprenticeships such as financial difficulties due to an insufficient household income, a lack of access to information and careers advice in schools, negative self-image and lack of parity of esteem reinforced by parents and teachers, relatively limited transferability of the apprenticeship qualification, prior qualifications making young people under or overqualified, a lack of access to apprentice role models and employers and lastly, an application process that is difficult to navigate.

The Strategy Behind Addressing the Barriers to Apprenticeships

Our strategy in addressing these barriers will include:

- Increasing awareness: This book is aimed at increasing awareness of apprenticeships to young people, in general, especially those from disadvantaged backgrounds of the many technical and vocational options available to them through apprenticeships, and why it could be the quickest route to help them acquire social and financial mobility, financial security and a more fulfilling and rewarding career if they make the right choices.

- Teaching young people how to develop "The most effective strategies on How to secure an apprenticeship within 1-3 months. Time scale depends on the effort.

- Informing you how you can go about searching for apprenticeships of your choice and where to look for apprenticeship opportunities.

Introduction

- Elaborating on effective techniques on how to apply for apprenticeships of choice and effective techniques on how to prepare for interviews using the STAR Approach to answer scenario-based questions from real-life examples, from the experiences of other clients who have successfully secured apprenticeships in various roles and sectors including business administration, tax, health and social care, investment banking – with the support of A & F Tutors Ltd.

- Addressing outdated perceptions amongst young people and parents, especially those from disadvantaged backgrounds such as apprenticeships being second-rate compared to going to university after college or that A-levels are the best route for all young people.

According to a survey carried out by A&F TUTORS Ltd (an education consulting firm aimed at promoting social mobility to children from a disadvantaged background, within the borough of Southwark where most of our clients are based), 95% of young people and parents do not know what

Introduction

apprenticeships are and how their child can benefit from it – believing the traditional route of going to university is always better because it offers the best career opportunities.

Based on our experience at A&F Tutors Ltd, there over thirty applications from graduates across the country for every tutoring role advertised by A & F Tutors Ltd. Furthermore, new research findings by Forbes Magazine shows that university is no longer the path to success because graduates and high school students who go down the apprenticeship route end up earning about the same over time, though an apprentice has a higher chance of becoming successful career-wise and financially because they would be debt-free from student loan payments whilst having the chance to start earning, saving and investing earlier – key factors for achieving financial security.

Unemployment of young people stifles the country's economic growth and lets down young people, especially those from poor backgrounds who are most in need of support and opportunities for growth and social mobility, therefore, the fundamental aim of this book is to encourage, educate, empower, guide and support young people, especially those from disadvantage background to get an apprenticeship of their choice, in line with their passion and strengths, could be the golden ticket to their child's financial and career success, if they use the opportunity wisely.

This is an important decision that can be a crucial crossroad in your life, as such, it's best that you're fully informed about the nature of apprenticeships so that you can make the best decision for yourself about your future.

What is an Apprenticeship Training?

An apprenticeship gives you practical on-the-job experience, essential learning tools and all-important qualifications that will last you a lifetime, wherever tomorrow takes you. An apprenticeship is also a real job. You will be working alongside experienced people, supporting them, and learning from them as you go. You will be working at least 30 hours a week, and you will gain most of the training you need in the workplace, but usually, you will combine work experience with attending a college, training provider, training centre or learn online to gain vital skills and

Introduction

qualifications. Generally, as an apprentice, you will spend 20% of your training working towards a qualification at college and 80% training on the job, but this depends on your provider and employer on what you will be doing, you could study at work, at home or go to college or university to get your qualification.

The decision whether to go for an apprenticeship or not should be informed, hence the need to understand its benefits. Apprenticeships are suitable for anybody at any age, although most people think they are just for school and college leavers. Whether you're looking to start your career after school or university, or you want to change your career route – apprenticeships are for everyone!

Many employers even put their current members of staff on apprenticeships to help them develop, this includes anything from management to engineering qualifications, so they learn the latest techniques!

Introduction

Why an Apprenticeship?

Apprenticeships offer young people the opportunities to achieve financial security and social mobility earlier, if they use the opportunity wisely, and addresses inequality: Whilst apprenticeship can provide long term, fulfilling careers. However, at present, because of a lack of awareness, young people, and their families, especially those from disadvantaged backgrounds, are still missing out on some of the best apprenticeship opportunities. For me, from the experience of mentoring young people get into apprenticeship programmes, and also how to use the opportunity wisely by saving and investing money, an apprenticeship is a golden opportunity, especially to those from disadvantaged backgrounds to achieve financial security and social mobility because it offers them an opportunity to start learning, earning, saving, and investing much earlier than usual. As said in the book, Richest Man in Babylon" by George. S. Clason – one of the best books on Personal Finance and Wealth Building" the most efficient and effective way to build financial wealth or achieve financial security is to "make money, keep money and invest money."

Introduction

Time also plays a critical role in building financial wealth, because the earlier you start making money, keeping money and investing money, the earlier you could become a millionaire and financially secure.

"The Power of Focus" by Jack Canfield, Mark Victor Hansen and Les Hewitt which teaches "How to hit your business, personal and financial targets with absolute certainty, confirms the importance of time and investing in gaining financial security. It states: "Starting at age 18, if you invest $100 or £100 every month compounded (compounded means you earn interest on interest) every year at 10%, you will have more than $1.1 million or £1.1 million pounds tucked away by the time you are 65". More information on how compound interest works, and how it can help you become a millionaire or acquire financial security and freedom can be found in my book on Amazon titled "How To Invest In The Stock Market For The First Time And Make Money". In simple terms, having the opportunity to start working, earning, and investing money means you stand a very good chance of becoming a millionaire by 65 or earlier (if you invest more than $100 or £100, earning 10% or more every year).

Introduction

An apprenticeship provides young people with the opportunity, to build valuable skills and get on the path to success. They will also have access to a workplace mentor who is someone that has lots of industry experience to support you through your job and qualification. Additionally, many apprenticeships are done alongside a qualification, so whether you are working towards a qualification equivalent to GCSEs or up to a master's level, you will get something! An apprenticeship can further provide workplace skills that help people develop the skills they need for the workplace and boost their job prospects, their long-term career progression, and earning potential!

Employers believe that apprentices are 15% more employable than those with other qualifications. Respected by employers across the world, an apprenticeship will lead to a national qualification, with a network of support available to give you all the help you need to do well. It's also in your employers' interest to help you succeed. All your training will be designed with your employer. So, you can relax in the knowledge that you're learning the right stuff to get you ahead.

Introduction

Whilst your mates who attended University would be leaving after 3 years with about £50,000 of debts from a student loan, no work experience and little or no employable skills, you will be miles ahead of them in many ways. You will have no student debt but still have earned a degree because your employer will pay for it plus you'll have about 3 plus years of work experience in the same field or sector, meaning better jobs and career opportunities for you. However, being successful in an apprenticeship means you have to overcome or deal with challenges linked to apprenticeships.

Challenges Of an Apprenticeship

Though an apprenticeship is a great way to enjoy a successful start in work, and life, learn the skills and gain the qualifications you want, gain confidence and the chance to learn while earning, every apprenticeship is different, varied, stimulating and but also has its challenges too. Your starting salary might be much lower than that of a graduate. However, many apprentices earn similar or better salaries than graduates depending on the job type and/or sector.

Some apprentices earn similar or better salaries than graduates depending on the job type and/or sectors like the NHS, engineering, and financial services. So, you should spend time doing your research well, know which sector you want to work in before applying.

You cannot gain access to certain careers through an apprenticeship route. Having an undergraduate degree will be an essential requirement for certain careers, particularly in areas such as medicine and science. If you do want to gain a higher qualification through an apprenticeship, it will take much longer and the range of courses you will be able to study might be more limited than if you applied with A-levels.

Starting salaries for graduates tend to be higher. A 2014 Labour Force Survey showed that, on average, those with a degree earn more money per hour than those with NVQ-level qualifications. But again, this does not apply in all cases. Level 3 apprenticeships and above with good employers like the local/central government, global companies like KPMG, Engineering, JP Morgan, Investment firms usually pay annual salaries of £18000 per year and above

Introduction

Having known that the experiences, development, and salary you will earn as an apprentice depends on the type of role, sector, apprenticeship level, it is critical you carry out detailed research to discover the apprenticeship type that's right for you.

Types Of Apprenticeship

In England, there are currently four levels of apprenticeship: intermediate

(level 2), advanced (level 3), higher (levels 4 & 5) and degree (levels 6 & 7). They all involve a work-based learning programme and lead to nationally recognised qualifications.

Intermediate (Level 2) Apprenticeships

What Are Intermediate Apprenticeships (Level 2)?

Level 2 Apprenticeships or Intermediate apprenticeships are the equivalents of getting 5 GCSEs at A* - C (or 9 to 4 on the new scales).

They are the most popular level apprenticeship in the UK and have been for years! They are a great way to take the first step in starting your future career, and for those aged 16, they offer an alternative to staying at school and learning in the traditional classroom environment.

At this level, you will be working full-time with an employer and spending time studying towards a qualification at college or with a training provider. You will study towards qualifications at the same level as five GCSEs, such as NVQ Level 2, and a knowledge-based qualification such as BTEC Diploma and Certificate, relevant to the sector and job role.

What Happens Next After a Level 2 Apprenticeship?

You can go on to complete advanced and higher apprenticeships. At level 2, your apprenticeship will be designed to train you for work to the best of your ability rather than focus on increasing your responsibility straight away, but this doesn't mean you won't have any. You will learn key employability skills as well as get specialised training with the company that you work for.

What Do I Need to Get a Level 2 Apprenticeship?

To get onto an intermediate apprenticeship, it is likely that you will need two or more GCSEs, although some employers don't ask for any formal qualifications. Instead, they ask if you have experience in the industry, if you don't have basic maths and English skills, you may have to complete a basic literacy and numeracy test to check that the level apprenticeship is right for you.

Can I Do a Level 2 Apprenticeship?

An intermediate apprenticeship is for anybody at any age, but due to the level of the qualification, they aren't suited to everybody. An intermediate apprenticeship is right for you if you don't have any GCSEs or equivalent qualifications or it has been a number of years since the last time you studied, and you'd like to train in a new industry. If you have GCSEs or lots of experience in the industry your ideal apprenticeship is in, you may be better suited to an advanced apprenticeship.

What Are Level 2 Apprenticeships Like?

You will be working like any other employee doing the exact same jobs with the same duties and responsibilities, you will just have more support. You will spend 80% of your time at work, whether that's on the workshop floor, working on reception, in the office or much more. As an intermediate apprentice, you will be spending 20% of your time training towards a qualification. The way this is organised will also depend on your employer, you might spend once a week training or you might spend block release working for weeks on end at the company and then spend a week at college training. You will also be working towards a qualification with the support of a workplace mentor, this might be your manager, someone else you work with, or it could be someone that's already done the programme.

How Much Do I Earn in a Level 2 Apprenticeship?

Studies conducted by A & F Tutors LTD, an education consulting, private tutoring and social mobility firm using various resources and job vacancy platforms including notgoingtouni.co.uk, getmyfirstjob.co.uk, government apprenticeship website, shows most level 2 apprenticeships pay salaries of about £130 up to £290 per week depending on the sector, location, industry, company.

What Qualification Do I Get?

You will get level 2 qualifications doing an intermediate apprenticeship, this means you'll get qualifications that are the equivalent to 5 good GCSEs, that's A* - C or 9-4. You might get BTECs or NVQs, depending on what apprenticeship you choose to do. If you do not have English or maths qualifications, you will also get level 2 Functional Skills in maths and English to pass the apprenticeship programme. Depending on your employer, you may also work on other qualifications which are more directly related to your job. That could be a qualification to use certain systems at your workplace or use certain pieces of machinery. It all depends on where you end up working!

What Does an Employer Look for In My Level 2 Apprenticeship Application?

The skills required in most apprenticeships by employers are different from one sector/job to another, but there are core skills needed in all jobs to build a successful career. The fundamental attribute needed in all Level 2 apprenticeships is your passion for the job for which you are applying. This is because they will not expect you to have a lot of or any experience, and in most cases, you do not need the experience to secure the apprenticeship, even though having experience could give you an advantage these days as apprenticeships are becoming more competitive. But if you can show you have good time management, can prioritise, and are organised this will get you a long way! Finally, you will need 3 or more GCSEs to get onto an intermediate apprenticeship too.

However, if you have more experience than most, this may not be as important – you will just have to pass some basic maths and numeracy tests before being enrolled on the course.

Summary of the Skills required for Level 2 - Intermediate Apprenticeship

- Passion for the job.

- Have good time management (you can prioritise tasks and are organised).

- Level 1 English and Maths.

- Enthusiasm – you are keen to learn.

What comes next after completing a level 2 apprenticeship?

After completing an intermediate apprenticeship, your options include:

- Moving into full-time employment in the company you completed your apprenticeship with.

- Applying for better jobs related to your intermediate apprenticeship qualification.

- Progressing onto a level 3 or advanced apprenticeship with a new or existing employer.

Level 3 – Advanced Apprenticeships – The equivalent of L3 BTECs at College or A-Levels

Advanced apprenticeships (Level 3) are suitable for those who want to earn money and want to get a degree or higher qualification after but do not want to go to university. Level 3 apprenticeships or advanced apprenticeships are the equivalent of you getting two good A-Level passes and come just after intermediate (level 2) apprenticeships.

These are a great opportunity for you after school if you have great GCSEs or even after college to get your foot in the door. Many employers streamline their apprenticeships starting at an advanced level.

What Will I Be Doing as An Advanced Apprentice?

As an advanced apprentice, you will be working full-time with an employer and spending time studying towards a qualification with a training provider or at college. You will study towards qualifications at the same level as two A-Level passes, such as NVQ Level 3, and a knowledge-based qualification such as BTEC Diploma and Certificate, relevant to the sector and job role. Some of these are also accredited by institutes depending on where you study – so you could be chartered in engineering or marketing and much more!

How Is a Level 3 Apprenticeship Designed?

Your apprenticeship will be designed to slowly start giving you more responsibility the further you get through your qualification and the more comfortable you get with your organisation. You could be managing areas of your team as an advanced apprentice! However, if you don't feel comfortable with lots of responsibility, your employer will offer you support to get to this point further down in your career.

You will also have specialist training with the company while learning key employability skills.

What Are They Like?

As an advanced apprentice, you will have the same responsibilities and duties as anyone in the same job as you, you will just have more support and spend some of your time training towards a qualification. Generally, time and training towards qualifications take around a quarter of your time. Training will either be at work, or you will go to college to study. The remainder of your time will be spent in your job, with the support of a workplace mentor. This could be your manager, someone else you work with or someone else who has already done the programme.

What Qualification Do I Get After an Advanced Apprenticeship Training?

You will get level 3 qualifications doing an advanced apprenticeship, this means you will get qualifications that are the equivalent to 2 A-level passes. You might get BTECs and/or NVQs, depending on what apprenticeship you choose to do. If you don't have English or maths qualifications, you will also get level 2 or 3 Functional Skills in maths and English to pass the apprenticeship programme. Depending on your employer, you may also work on other qualifications which are more directly related to your job. That could be a qualification to use certain systems at your workplace or use certain pieces of machinery. It all depends on where you end up working!

How Do They Work?

As mentioned above, as an advanced apprentice, you will be spending around a quarter of your time training towards a qualification. How you spend this time will vary depending on your employer, you might have in-house training, or you could go to an external training provider or college. The way this is organised will also depend on your employer, you might spend once a week training or you might spend block release working for weeks on end at the company and then spend a week at college training.

38

Can I do An Advanced or Level 3 Apprenticeship?

To do an advanced apprenticeship, you will probably need to have three or more GCSEs, but some employers will ask for one or two A-levels too. Other employers will not ask for any formal qualifications but may just ask for you to have previous experience in the industry the apprenticeship is in. To get onto an advanced apprenticeship, it is likely that you will need some formal qualifications. You could have done an intermediate apprenticeship, got more than 5 GCSEs or some A-Level passes. Alternatively, if you have a lot of experience in the industry, you may just need to pass a few basic English and maths tests.

What Kind of Apprenticeships Can You Do at Level 3?

Across any sector, in any company – so long as they are being offered.

What Does an Employer Look for In My Application and What Skills Do I Need to Get an Advanced Apprenticeship?

An employer will be looking for your passion for the organisation, the apprenticeship and that you can envision your career progressing in that industry. What employers are not looking for is a long list of employment history, but a part-time job will be something that improves your application. Most employers will also be looking for other ways that you can show time management, prioritisation, and skills suitable for the workplace. From my experience in my role as an apprenticeship and career mentor, to get into a good position and to get an advanced apprenticeship now that advanced apprenticeships are more competitive with about 100 applications per role in good roles and for good companies, you will need two A levels, previous part-time or full-time job experience, plus you need to show passion for the organisation, apprenticeship, role, including the ability to demonstrate time management, prioritisation and other work-based soft skills like problem-solving, et cetera, depending on the job type. Statistics from our experiences of providing career mentoring to clients at A&F Tutors Ltd showed candidates who could demonstrate passion, had support from a career mentor and 60% of the above skills secured an apprenticeship within 1-3 months of interviews. However, those who could not demonstrate these skills in interviews, especially passion for the role, apprenticeship and company struggled to secure a suitable role and took much longer than 6 months. The role of mentors and how to demonstrate key skills required for apprenticeships will be discussed later.

Higher Apprenticeships (Level 4 +)

Higher apprenticeships are the level after advanced apprenticeships and could offer you a variety of qualifications. They range from the equivalent to the first year of an undergraduate degree (level 4) all the way to postgraduate (level 7). As a higher apprentice, you will be spending 20% of your working week studying towards a qualification at college or with a training provider and 80% working.

You will be working towards one of the following levels 4, 5, 6 or 7 qualifications, depending on what level apprenticeship you choose.

Level 4 Apprenticeships

These are the equivalent to an HNC, CertHE, Level 4 NVQ, BTEC or first year of university.

Requirements for an ACA accounting Level 4 apprenticeship role could look something like:

- Qualification Required: BBB grade from 3 A levels, B grade or above in GCSE Maths and English

- Job Specific Skills Required: Excellent Numeracy and Good IT skills

- Personal Qualities Required: Articulate, Confident with Good Communication Skills

Requirements for pre-employment Level 4 software engineering apprenticeship could look something like:

- Qualifications Required: 5 GCSEs C – A* including Maths and English

- Qualifications Required: Level 3 Qualifications (BTEC, NVQ or Equivalent)

- Experience: 3 months prior coding knowledge

- Skills Required: Good attention to detail, logical approach to problem-solving, ability to manage complex tasks and meet datelines.

- Personal Qualities: Good communication and interpersonal skills, able to work in a team, able to under impact of the functionality on customer/appreciate customer needs

However, this may be different from one job industry to another. Regardless of the differences, the above qualifications, some work experience, and soft skills such as teamwork, problem-solving skills, ability to communicate well, great interpersonal skills etc, and more, depending on the industry are required.

Level 5 Apprenticeships

These are the equivalent to a DipHE, HND, Level 5 NVQ, Level 5 BTEC, foundation degree or second year of university.

Requirements for Level 5 Apprenticeships

If you are currently at school, college, or sixth form, you must be completing three A levels, five Highers or equivalent qualifications, in advance of the programme start date. If you are now working, you must have attained three A levels, five Highers or equivalent qualifications. You must also have achieved Level 2/GCSE qualification (or equivalent) in English Language and Mathematics. Do take note that in some high-level apprenticeships, depending on the sector, no qualifications or experience are required as long as you are determined to have a long-term career in that sector and can manage yourself well.

Level 7 Apprenticeships

These are the equivalent to an MEng, MA, MSc, Level 7 NVQ, PGCSE or Postgraduate certificate, as such, there is an academic barrier to entry on these apprenticeships. These will be at least level 3 qualifications, this could be an advanced apprenticeship, A-Levels, BTEC or NVQ. Industry experience can also sometimes substitute for recent qualifications. As a higher apprentice, you will hold a position in an organisation that has a lot of responsibility. You shouldn't be put off by this, you will have support from your manager and by your workplace mentor to make sure you are not overwhelmed. You could even be managing your own team or processes by the end of the programme!

You'll be learning key employability skills as well as getting specialist training from the employer. At the end of your apprenticeship, you could go onto a higher-level apprenticeship or go to university. You might have had enough of studying for qualifications and just go onto a full-time position at an organisation.

What Are They Like?

If you do a higher apprenticeship, you'll have support from your manager, workplace mentor and tutor. After your initial induction period, you will be given a lot of responsibility as a higher apprentice, with continued support. You could be managing teams, projects, or processes at your company within the first few months of your placement! For 20% of the week, you will be either at work studying or at college, university or a training provider working towards your qualification. As such, you'll spend most of your week with a workplace mentor.

What Qualification Do I Get?

The type of qualification that you get with a higher apprenticeship will depend on what level of apprenticeship you choose to do. It could be anything from the equivalent to a foundation degree all the way up to a postgraduate qualification!

Here is some more information about the qualifications you could get:

- Level 4 Apprenticeships – HNC, CertHE, Level 4 NVQ, BTEC or first year of university.

- Level 5 Apprenticeships – DipHE, HND, Level 5 NVQ, Level 5 BTEC, foundation degree or second year of university.

- Level 6 Apprenticeships – BA or BSc Degree, Graduate Certificate, Level 6 NVQ or BTEC.

- Level 7 Apprenticeships – Meng, MA, MSc, Level 7 NVQ, PGCSE or Postgraduate certificate.

You will have to get your Level 2 or 3 Functional Skills qualification as well to pass the apprenticeship programme if you don't have recent qualifications in English and maths.

Depending on your employer, you may also work on other qualifications which are more directly related to your job. This could include training for job-specific machinery. It all depends on where you end up working!

What Kind of Apprenticeships Can You Do at A Higher Level?

All types from level 1 to level 7 in all sectors.

What Does an Employer Look for In My Application?

At this point, any kind of employment experience would serve you well to prove to your employer your commitment skills to a job, otherwise emphasise to the employer that you have time-management skills and can work efficiently under pressure. An employer will also be looking for a passion for the organisation, apprenticeship, and the industry. They will want to know that you are a high achiever as higher apprenticeships can be challenging due to their academic nature, and they wouldn't want you to struggle with the qualification.

Are These Graduate Apprenticeships?

You could refer to a level 7 apprenticeship as a graduate apprenticeship or graduate programme. This is because you will need a degree or degree level qualification to get onto the course. You will leave this apprenticeship with a postgraduate qualification and lots of experience!

By supporting young people to gain skills and work experience through paid apprenticeships, we are addressing barriers to, and improving social mobility for young people, especially those who are less well off because they do not have a family member or social network to get a foot on the "career ladder" with high calibre employers. Nothing teaches a young person about the realities of life, how, when and why they should grow up, whilst making valuable contributions to society better than an apprenticeship.

How Do I Secure an Apprenticeship in Line with My Passion and Skills?

An apprenticeship is a real job and could be a solid foundation for a successful career. Passion is defined as having a very strong emotion for something, but this emotion can be controlled. Therefore, a job that you have a passion for, would be one that you have a strong desire to do and enjoy doing, evening if you are not earning money for doing that job. For example, when I began my career in investment banking in 2012, I did private tutoring and mentoring free of charge for more than 2 years to family friends, on the side. The reason being, it gave me an inner glow of satisfaction that I was making a positive contribution to people's lives, which I could measure or quantify because I could see the impact of my support on their growth plan. But at that time as an analyst in investment banking, I was in my dream job for two reasons. First I had paid £21000 in fees alone, not factoring in other costs, to attend one of the top business schools in London, UK and the world to study a specialist master's in financial engineering and Quantitative Finance (MSc in Mathematical Trading and Finance at Cass Business School, London).

This is because I had a dream to become an investment banker, make lots of money quickly and retire early, say within three to five years. Hence securing the analyst job with a starting salary of £35000 without bonuses, was a dream come true and a good return on investment – mindful of the fact that I had spent more than £20,000 towards fees, savings from a five-year job as a customer service assistant with the railway. However, I did not enjoy being in that environment due to the nature of the job, such as working crazy hours and could not measure the direct positive impact of my action on people's lives. Instead, I felt I was a "slave" to money, whose main job was to fix computers/networks to ensure traders and banks make money. At this point, there was a collision between my dream job and reality. Because I needed the money to pay for student loans, debts and survive, I stayed in investment banking for a few years, unhappy, though competent and did well in my various roles. 2014, was the turning point. As said earlier, I still maintained my part-time private tutoring role whilst working as an analyst in investment banking. One afternoon after work, I met one of my students as I was walking home after work. I supported him to prepare for Year 6 SATS and the results were out.

As he came closer, and we made eye contact, he ran fast towards me, gave me a big hug, with tears in his eyes and thanked me for the support I had given him. I had never felt that happy and satisfied regarding the impact of my actions on someone's life for a long time, before that day, was very emotional. That was the day I realised my passion or what motivates me was any job that made a positive impact on people's lives which was in line with my values – I realised tutoring and mentoring were. I resigned immediately from investment banking.

When deciding your career make sure you identify a job or industry you're passionate about, and apply for it, if you are not sure, apply for jobs you believe you have the skills for. Assuming we have an average of 12 hours of being active every day from Monday to Friday, from 6 am g when we wake up to 6 pm when we finish work, and assuming you start work at 9 am as an apprentice to finish at 5/6 pm, implies you spend an average of 8 to 9 hours out of your 12 active hours at work, excluding travelling time. 8 out of 12 hours at work means we spend almost 70% of our active hours every day at work.

Moreso, in other roles like medical positions and carers in care homes it is 12 hours shift, similar to those working in roles like trading in investment banks. Therefore, if you are doing a job you are not passionate about or related to something you are passionate about and in line with your values you will not be motivated to do your job well, work hard and do your best. Consequently, you will become an ineffective team member, making it difficult for you to fit within your team and before you know, you will either leave the job for another job, which may end up being a vicious cycle. To conclude, what we do to earn money takes up 70 - 80% of our lives, on average. Therefore, if we want to stay happy 70-80% of the time every day in active lifestyles, we need to take time to identify what we are passionate about and what is in line with the skills we have or can learn, from there we can channel all our energy and effort into that, believing even when it is difficult to believe that we will succeed.

Do not worry about money because when you do what you are passionate about, making sufficient money to meet your needs and wants becomes a natural by-product of your job or trade.

This is because when you are passionate about something, you will eventually become the "best" at it with time, and when you are the best in providing a service or product – demand for it will increase exponentially with time.

Obviously, the next question should you be asking is:

How do I find the job, apprenticeship, or business I am passionate about?

How I Found My Passion

I found my passion in two ways. First working in investment banking made me realise that was not a place for me in the long term, hence triggering the need to find what I was passionate about. Though I was in investment banking, I did not abandon private tutoring and mentoring because I had my greatest satisfaction from it. In simple terms, I found my passion by exploring different roles: tutoring/mentoring alongside investment banking job.

The advantage of exploring different roles, especially when you are younger, as an apprentice, exposes you to a variety of roles and experiences.

It also gives you a birds-eye view of different tasks and jobs you gained happiness and satisfaction from, during your work experiences, placement etc upon reflection. At this point, you can make an informed and better decision of what you enjoy doing or your passionate about.

Secondly, you can find your passion by reflecting on strengths and weaknesses at school, college, and previous jobs. This can be achieved by making notes of the different subjects you did, topics you enjoyed most and why. Do the same for any work experience you have had, which aspects you enjoyed doing and which you did not. Find if there is any link between the subject you enjoyed at school and any job or work experience you had, if there is a link between both in terms of satisfaction and competency, then that is most likely your passion. For example, if you had A grades in mathematics, you are more likely to enjoy working in tax, finance and a number of related roles as opposed to something like IT, because these roles are in line with your strengths

On reflection, my best results in school and University were in mathematics. After completing my master's in mathematics, I would have had a more productive and happy life if I went on to become a maths teacher or lecturer straight away than going into investment banking. I loved maths at school, college, and University, and also enjoyed sharing my knowledge a lot during my private tutoring roles. So, there was a relationship between what subject I enjoyed doing at school and what I enjoyed during my role as a tutor. Also, a role as a trader or quantitative analyst would have been more enjoyable for me in investment banking because maths was my key strength and an essential requirement in these roles. So, working in a hybrid IT role rather than Maths related role in investment banking was not the best option for me because it was not in line with my key strengths.

Next is to look for suitable apprenticeships in companies whose values are in line with yours. For example, being someone who enjoys helping others and seeing them grow, in hindsight, working for a company like Bloomberg would have been more satisfying and rewarding for me because their values are in line with mine (aimed at making a positive contribution to people's lives in the community). Eighty per cent of the company's profits goes back to the community to support charitable work.

Once the decision on what type of roles and companies you're aiming to work have been made, it is time to create a professional CV and cover letter. Register on apprenticeship opportunities websites for regular updates on jobs every week. It is also a good habit to visit the company's website and check for apprenticeships if you are interested in working for them or are already working there and considering an apprenticeship, visit the company's jobs board, check for apprenticeships, and apply directly. Experience has taught me that direct applications from company websites increases your chance of securing an interview if done properly and early enough because most people visit or rely on Google searches or Indeed. By the time these jobs are advertised there, you may not have enough time left to apply and most applicants go through this route, which makes it very competitive and job openings may have closed.

Select two similar suitable jobs every week, take your time to prepare your CV and cover letter or personal statement to show you are capable of doing the job – that you meet all or most person specifications.

The effectiveness of your applications is not based on the number of applications you make every week but on the effort you put in to ensure that you can show that your skills and knowledge satisfies most if not all the person's specification. If you apply for any job that comes your way, you would be ineffective because you would not put in the time and effort required to ensure your CV & cover letter meets the personal specifications of the job. You should avoid applying to more positions than you are able to keep track of, in case you receive a call, you would find it difficult to reconcile which application it was – which does not go down well with employers – too many applications make the process confusing and difficult to track. Finally, applying for a few, but similar roles is critical because most of the time, the interview questions in similar roles will overlap. The more interviews you have for jobs in that role, the higher the chances you will do well in the next interview if you used your last interview experience to prepare.

For example, if you want an accounting level 3 apprenticeship, it is better to stick to accounting level apprenticeships only. reason being most or some of the questions in all interviews linked to your applications will be similar. So, the more interviews you get, the higher your chances of securing an apprenticeship earlier because you will come across technical, personal, and accounting-based questions that you have heard before in previous interviews. Arguably, from experience, this could be the most important strategy on how to increase your chances of securing a job or apprenticeship of choice within the shortest possible time.

"Confronting the brutal facts in life [such as] challenges, is one of the best ways to make that transition from mediocrity to excellence, or from good to great"

– Jim Collins (Author of "Good to Great")

How To Develop an Effective CV, Cover Letter and Personal Statement

One of the best ways to teach someone how to do or to learn something is to use examples or case studies. On that note, I would like to share a copy of a professional CV and cover letter developed by career mentors at A&F Tutors for Business administration LEVEL 3 apprenticeship mentees, who ended up securing an interview for the role, and the apprenticeship, thanks to our continuous support with mock interview preparations as well. Mentors at A&F Tutors Ltd has supported teenagers and adults into apprenticeships.

- One of our apprenticeship mentees, a teenager, with BTEC, works with Southwark Council, whilst studying towards his level 3 certificate in Business Administration. This is equivalent to A levels, after which he can go on to Level 4 certificate, equivalent to first-year University, then to level 5, and finally 6 which is equivalent to a degree – as discussed earlier. This apprenticeship gives him the opportunity to get a degree free of charge because the employer pays for

How To Develop an Effective CV, Cover Letter and Personal Statement

his studies but is getting paid on top of that whilst gaining work experience. In simple terms, he gets paid for studying, whilst gaining vital experience, skills, and knowledge for a successful career in Business Administration, Finance etc. More so, at level 4, he will achieve a level 4 and 5, he will secure a level 4 certificate and a diploma at level 5, then a degree at level 6.

- Similarly, our second apprenticeship mentee, also a teenager with A level Economics and English, recently secured a Level 3 apprenticeship role as an employment and skills apprentice at Lewisham College.

- The third, this one being an adult, recently secured a Nursing Associate Level 4 Apprenticeship with Kings College Hospital London – Thanks to the support of our able team at A & F Tutors Ltd.

Since the Business Administration apprenticeships are similar, I will share only a copy of the CV and cover letter/personal

How To Develop an Effective CV, Cover Letter and Personal Statement

statement used in both roles and nursing associate copies, since the role is different from the other two.

How To Develop an Effective CV, Cover Letter and Personal Statement

Original Copy of a Client's cv for Employment and Skills Level 3 Apprenticeship

[NAME IN CAPITAL LETTERS AND BOLD]

[ADDRESS]

Tel: [Mobile and home phone number]

Email: [Email]

PROFILE

A hard-working individual, who has completed work experience at Barclays Banks, achieved an A grade in GCSE Mathematics, B grade in English and currently studying Economics and English at A-Levels; with a passion to develop a career in the education sector. Currently working as a volunteer business administrator for A&F Tutors Ltd. A good listener who is intellectually curious and can work well on my own and as part of a team. Have a strong track record in delivering great customer service whilst contributing to the overall performance of a team. A quick learner with a "can-do attitude" with the ability to prioritise and manage workload with conflicting demands. Looking for apprenticeship opportunities in a challenging and rewarding environment to learn and grow, such as business and finance.

QUALIFICATIONS AND ACHIEVEMENTS

Duke of Edinburgh: Bronze award

I am currently attending City and Islington College where I am studying Economics and English. So far, I can say that school has taught me a lot of valuable skills in dealing with people and everyday tasks such as collaboration and leadership skills. I am working very hard to make sure that I achieve the best grades I can possibly get to facilitate my future career prospects in higher education.

GCSE: English Language: B   Additional Science: C
English Literature: B   History: C
Maths: A   Core Science: C

KEY SKILLS

- Intellectually curious with good research skills, accuracy, and attention to detail.

- Target driven and able to use my own initiative to get things done to meet any deadline.

- Strong interpersonal skills along with superb oral and written communication skills, flexible to new ideas.

- Capable of following procedures, systematic processes alongside being methodical and accurate approach to work activities.

- Skilful at finding solutions to issues and problems solving

- Positive attitude, energetic approach and self-motivated.

- Capable of influencing the opinions of customers while being able to handle complaints, aggressive customers, and difficult situations.

EMPLOYMENT HISTORY

A&F Tutors   **Jan 2019 - Current**

Job Title: Business/Admin Support Officer (Volunteer)

- Providing daily support to ensure clients via email, phone, or face to face in order to ensure receive top-quality customer service.

- Updating spreadsheets of clients and student records, monitoring emails, returning calls, booking new sales leads and developing files for new students.

- Assist in the creation and distribution of marketing materials

- Dealing with customer queries by email, reviewing student performance.

- Assist in the preparation of stock market trading materials for training.

- Publishing Stock market trading tips on LinkedIn.

- Booking new clients and carrying out inductions.

- Building, maintaining and updating a database of clients.

- Calculating payments made for lessons, hours, and monthly profit and loss.

Specsavers   **Sept 2017 – Jan 2019**

Job Title: Customer Service Assistant

- Maintaining high standards of cleanliness and orderliness in all public areas.

- Front of house, meeting, greeting and serving customers.

- Informing customers of collection times or delivery times and dates.

- Resolving disputes and customer complaints in a polite manner.

- Highlighting special offers and promotions to customers.

- Providing product advice, knowledge and guidance to customers.

- Using the till for payment transactions and processing credit card payments.

- Adhering to company policies, processes and procedures, and ethos

- Filing and Organising Data and Handling sensitive and private customer information.

- Attending to deliveries and sorting them out to the right department.

Peckham All Saints Church   Jul 2016 – Sept 2016

Job Title: Junior Apprentice

- Assisting the coordinator to organise the children in teams for daily activities.

- Answering the phone, dealing with parents' inquiries and passing to the right person.

- Attending meetings, minutes taking and coming up with new topic ideas for the team.

- Assisting with proof-reading, copying, packing, posting promotional materials

- Taking part in the debate team and winning the Southeast team.

Barclays Bank   **May 2016 (Two weeks)**

Job Title: Work Experience/Shadowing

- Understanding the banking world and Barclays bank as an individual.
- Attending conferences on the Banks current status.
- Learning about individual sectors of the bank and how they operate.
- Leaning about front-line customer service.

Greenwich Free School   **Sept 2014 – June 2015**

Job Title: School Voice

- Attending meetings with parents, teachers and pupils.
- Acting as a liaison between the pupils and the teachers.
- Helping to establish rules.
- Being a voice of the younger pupils and standing against bullying.
- School Ambassador on an open day.

- Featuring on the school magazine for achieving the most house points in my year.

HOBBIES

I enjoy current affairs, going out networking and meeting new people and learning something new. I love spending and making memories with friends and family.

How To Develop an Effective CV, Cover Letter and Personal Statement

Breakdown of What Makes a Good CV

Profile: Your CV profile should highlight, briefly, key work experiences you have had, grades at GCSEs and A level or any other academic qualifications especially, if it is related to the job you are applying for. It is also important to indicate that your future career interests are in line with the apprenticeship you are applying for. For example, if you want a career in mechanical engineering, indicate this and your desire to build a career in mechanical engineering. Apprenticeships are becoming very competitive these days, as more students/parents are becoming aware of its benefits – take your apprenticeship application seriously so you can stand out. You need to make sure your CV highlights your key skills, knowledge and qualification related to the role to save employers time and increase your chances of securing an interview with the employer.

For example, in the business administration apprenticeship application, I highlighted the client's excellent performance in Maths at GCSE, his administrative experience working with A&F TUTORS – an education consulting firm and key skills

How To Develop an Effective CV, Cover Letter and Personal Statement

gained in this experience - which were relevant to that role of employment and skills apprenticeship. So, if you are applying for an IT apprenticeship, and did ICT at GCSE and or computer science at A-LEVEL, you need to highlight these aspects in your profile, then articulate it in your cover letter or explain in detail using examples and in line with the STAR approach, which will be discussed further on in the book.

Be sure to use "active words" such as verbs and talk in the first person (first-person pronouns such as I/me/mine) in your CV and cover letter. Being in an administrative role, I also ensured only aspects related to administrative tasks in the applicant's CV were highlighted to ensure there is an overlap between the job specification and his past experience, though all other duties and responsibilities can be included.

You will still have the opportunity, to talk discuss key aspects of your CV that are relevant to the role you are applying for in your cover letter or personal statement – so do not create a CV longer than 2 pages or a maximum of 3 pages.

The table below shows how to match job specification in the apprenticeship role you are applying for using your

How To Develop an Effective CV, Cover Letter and Personal Statement

past/current experience in your CV - using a real-life example of how mentors at A&F Tutors Ltd supported the applicant to prepare his CV, apply, prepare for interviews and secure a level 3 business apprenticeship recently with Southwark Council and Lewisham College.

EMPLOYMENT AND SKILLS APPRENTICE ROLE	APPRENTICE'S CV
MAIN DUTIES OF APPRENTICESHIP ROLE 1. Update Access database with referrals from partner organisations, Update Word document for a monthly	**MAIN DUTIES OF APPLICANT AS A Business/Admin Support Officer AT A&F TUTORS LTD** 1. Updating spreadsheet of clients and student records, building, maintaining and updating a database of clients. 2. Monitoring emails and returning calls, booking

newsletter to partners, Update Access database with PLR information for learners 2. Monitor the team voicemail inbox and return calls or pass on messages as appropriate, contact learners when absent from class 3. Receive and answer emails as appropriate, take minutes of team meetings, type	new sales leads 3. Providing daily support to ensure clients via email, phone or face to face in order to ensure receive top-quality customer service 4. Contacting parents and clients regularly to book lessons, update them on changes affecting planned lessons such as when a tutor is absent 5. Booking new clients and carrying out inductions and preparing student files and archiving them 6. Photocopying/printing of materials and mail

How To Develop an Effective CV, Cover Letter and Personal Statement

them up and circulate to team members via email 4. Answer telephone calls from referring partners and take referral details accordingly 5. Contact Jobcentre Plus offices to ensure learners are remotely signed 6. Make up learner files and Archive learner files 7. Support	handling. 7. Maintaining contact with customer queries by email, reviewing student performance 8. Assist in the preparation of stock market trading materials for training 9. Publishing Stock market trading tips on LinkedIn. 10. Assist in the creation and distribution of marketing materials 11. Calculating payments made for lessons, hours, and monthly profit and loss

inductions and enrolments 8. Make up learner packs 9. Photocopying and printing documents as required 10. Any other duties as required	

Comparative Analysis of the Main Duties of the Advertised Role and Applicant's CV

In the table above, please take note of the active words such as "update", "support", "monitor", "provide", "contacting", "photocopying" were used when developing the applicant's CV. I also made sure that most of the active words in the applicant's cv to describe his duties in his previous role were synonymous with those used in the job description of the

How To Develop an Effective CV, Cover Letter and Personal Statement

advertised apprenticeship role. Most importantly, I made sure the duties in the apprentice's administrative role overlapped with those of the advertised role before taking a decision to apply plus his experience is in the education sector, in line with apprenticeship too. This means when building your CV to apply for a particular apprenticeship role or job, be sure to use experience which is similar to the role you are applying for and do your best to ensure that you can demonstrate that the duties in the role you are applying for overlaps with your existing or previous role, if any, by using the appropriate active words and duties your experience which overlaps with the duties of the advertised job. Doing this will make life easier for the employer to see immediately that you are a "good fit" for the job quickly, save the interviewers time and increase your chances of being called up for an interview.

In the scenario that you do not have experience which overlaps with the role you are applying for, that is fine – it does not really matter to an extent – rather focus on demonstrating how the skills and knowledge you gained at school/college or volunteering align with the skill/knowledge requirements of the role. Plus, as an apprentice, you will be trained and supported

How To Develop an Effective CV, Cover Letter and Personal Statement

to do the job as long as you have the passion for the job and to build a career in the sector. As such, you could use any past job experience through which you have gained core apprenticeship skills required such as teamwork, effective communication skills alongside examples in school or volunteering projects which shows that you have a passion for the job you are applying for – all that matters is that you secure the interview as that's the first step to getting the job.

However, some job applications such as applications to local councils, government departments and schools, require both a CV and personal statement to complete as part of an application form, this was the case in the employment and skills apprenticeship role described above. A personal statement gives you an opportunity to show (using examples) why you are the best fit for the job and organisation. The best way to do this is by using examples in your school, college and/or work experience to explain how and why you are the best person for that job. the most effective way to do this is to pay close attention to the person's specification of the job, every advertised job has a personal specification – simply a

How To Develop an Effective CV, Cover Letter and Personal Statement

summary of the key skills, knowledge, experience and values the employer is looking for in the applicant.

A person specification is usually split into two groups – essential skills, knowledge and experience and desirable skills, knowledge and experience, essential skills are denoted with (e) and desirable skills with (d) – the figure below shows essential and desirable skills for the admin apprentice role.

Person Specification	
Job Title	Administrator Apprentice
Education/ Qualifications	**Level 1 Business Administration (D)** **Working towards a Level 1 in English and Maths** At GCSE, I passed English Language [B], additional science [C], English Literature [B], Maths [A], History [C] and Core Science [C].

How To Develop an Effective CV, Cover Letter and Personal Statement

Knowledge	**Understand how to deal effectively with a range of clients and customers (E)**
	In my past and current roles, I have acquired the ability to effectively deal with a range of clients and customers. For example, I dealt effectively with unhappy customers by listening carefully to their complaints or requests, apologising for what had happened, reassuring the customer I will do my best to solve the problem and being proactive to prevent similar situations from reoccurring. For example, in my role as a business administrative staff at A & F Tutors Ltd, a customer rang complaining that the tutor arrived 30minutes late for lessons and she was very unhappy as it delayed her next appointment. I listened carefully to her, apologised for what happened. Asked her to give me 20 minutes to ring the tutor and find out why the lateness, and he confirmed that he struggled to find the address as it was his first time going there and also there was traffic. I called the client, explained the situation and reassured her it

will not happen again because I will keep in touch with the tutor to make sure he leaves homemaking reasonable allowances for any delays. She was satisfied with my reply and appreciated it.

In general, the ability to deal effectively with a range of clients requires empathy, respect, treating clients without discrimination regardless of their age, gender, cultural or religious background in line with the Equality Act 2010. It also means being sensitive to the needs and requirements of clients when serving them and making sure those who are disabled have access to the same and even better quality of service as others.

Knowledge of apprenticeships (D) [it gives me the opportunity to earn, learn and develop employable skills]

Through personal research and apprenticeship workshops at school, I have learnt that apprenticeships provide young people with the

	opportunity to earn, learn and gain qualifications without accruing debts on student loans. It gives me the opportunity to gain knowledge, experience and valuable employable skills in my area of choice earlier on in life. Therefore, this apprenticeship opportunity, for me is a golden opportunity to earn, learn, gain experience, knowledge and skills whilst making a meaningful impact on the growth of my team and the community. It also provides an unrivalled platform for me to develop steadily in line with my abilities and strengths.
Experience	**Experience in providing a general administration service (E)** • **Experience in using ICT and software packages, including Microsoft Office (Word, Excel, Outlook etc.) (E) [See cover letter].**

I use Microsoft Office in particular Word, Excel and PowerPoint to update spreadsheets, write reports and communicate with clients. For example, in my current role as a volunteer administrative assistant, I use Excel to develop and update spreadsheets of clients, carrying out data input of clients' names, emails, addresses, student's names, year in school, etc. This has given me an Advanced knowledge of Microsoft Office Packages.

- **Experience in producing letters and reports (E) [see cover letter]**
- Excellent command of Microsoft office packages (E)

In my current role and previous roles, I have developed the experience of writing business letters in line with business objectives. For example, in my current role with A & F Tutors Ltd, I regularly establish communication and working relationship with potential new customers by replying to their letters promptly in response to their enquiry such as cost of lesson per hour, which subjects we specialise in, payment structure etc via email using Outlook or drafting letters in Microsoft Word. I use Word and Excel to write reports of students' performance and improvements regularly in order to update parents on the impact of our tutoring service.

- **Experience of working in a busy, customer-focused environment (E) [see cover letter]**

For example, part of my role at A & F Tutors Ltd includes providing daily support to ensure clients via email, phone or face to face ensure receive top-quality customer service, Updating spreadsheet of clients and student records, Monitoring emails and returning calls, booking new sales leads, Developing files for new students, Assist in the creation and distribution of marketing materials, Dealing with customer queries by email, reviewing student performance, Assist in the preparation of stock market trading materials for training, Publishing Stock market trading tips on LinkedIn, Booking new clients and carrying out inductions, Building, maintaining and updating a database of clients, Calculating payments made for lessons, hours, and monthly profit and loss. Also, the experience of managing challenging customers whilst providing excellent customer service in my past and current experience has given me a good understanding of value for customer service.

Experience in working within the Further Education sector

A&F Tutors Ltd, the company I work for at the moment, is a provider of tutoring, apprenticeship,

	mentoring and financial education services to students and adults in further education. I have over 2 years experience of working in Further Education which I enjoy a lot. I am passionate about adding value to students' lives to help them meet their academic and career goals, therefore this role gives me the opportunity to fulfil that passion and build on existing further education experience.
Skills	• Excellent oral and written communication skills (E) Through academic and work experience, I have developed Excellent written and oral communication skills. I have developed this through the experience writing essays, reports and articles in Year 11 and A level English course works, which I passed with a B grade.

This has been enhanced by the experience of listening carefully to the needs of clients, providing the service required to meet their needs and being proactive to address issues before it becomes a problem. Through the experience of presentations, I have developed the ability to communicate to diverse audiences without audience fright, further developing my oral communication skills.

- A well-developed sense of diplomacy and tact (E)
- An ability to work collaboratively (E)

Having a sense of diplomacy and being tactful is important in any professional role and I have developed these values through personal and professional development by picking a non-stressful time to discuss issues with colleagues, always starting with positive comments when giving bad news and finding ways to compromise with others when required. Collaboration is important because it makes teamwork a reality.

Teamwork: Further, the experience of participating actively in group courses works and work experiences has also enabled me to gain essential team working skills. Teamwork is important because it compensates for individual weaknesses and enables the team/organisation to meet its goals. **For example, during my work experience as an apprentice, I assisted my team members by coming in early to cover shifts when required, mentored other trainees, staying at work longer than expected as required by the manager whenever I was required to do so – which I believe I would be required to do in abundance in this role, if successful.** I understand that becoming a successful investment professional also requires the ability to communicate well with others.

- Willingness to undertake appropriate training and development programmes (E)

I am more than willing to undertake any training and development program to improve my skills and ability to carry out my job.

- Ability to take the initiative (E) Ability to work with minimum supervision and work proactively (E)

At A & F Tutors, I was always proactive to identify issues customers could face. For example, a customer called asking about tutoring prices only and promised to call later for more. I figured out that usually, customers who do that may not likely call back if the price is too high for them. To provide more information to the customer why we charge that fee per hour and what they are getting

	to convince him to sign on, I asked for his email, and send more information with a breakdown of everything we offer during our tutoring session, also showing how we provide more for less money than our competitors, via email. He called back later on, confirmed he was impressed with the offer and price and signed up for our services.
Personal Qualities	- A passion for customer service (E) Good interpersonal skills (E) - prioritise workloads and meet deadlines (E) - Ability to work under pressure (E) I have demonstrated excellent customer service by being friendly and approachable to customers, listening to their needs, taking the right action to address them and being proactive to address issues before it becomes a problem. Moreso, I developed excellent interpersonal skills by

developing the ability to listen to people's views first which makes them feel valued, empathise, respect their values, be polite when sharing my views, and be sensitive to their needs.

To prioritise workload and meet datelines, I use a diary to categorise workloads into urgent, important and ordinary, including their dates, then juggle between them based on time and effort required whilst setting reminders close to dates to ensure I do not miss datelines. Juggling these personal and academic and professional datelines put me under a lot of pressure, but in the end, I was able to meet all coursework and professional datelines.

- A commitment to maintaining the principles of equality and diversity (E)

I will maintain equality and diversity in this role like in previous roles by working in line with the Equality Act 2010. This means treating everyone equally during service provision and without

How To Develop an Effective CV, Cover Letter and Personal Statement

> discrimination regardless of their race, sex, ethnic background. It also means ensuring everyone has access to services and taking action to ensure that happens. This is done in recognition of the fact that there are inequalities in society and actions need to be taken to address them.

Your main focus should be to ensure you demonstrate in your personal statement or cover letter how you meet the essential skills for the role first, before the desirable skills, the reason for this being that the essential skills are more important to the employer and that is what they will focus on more, in making that decision to call you for an interview.

How do I Prepare Effectively for My Interview?

Interview Preparation

Interview preparation is the most critical step in your journey to secure an apprenticeship or a job because it gives you the opportunity to demonstrate to your employers why you are the most suitable person for that role.

Do your research about the company – what are its products, services, culture, values and what makes it different from its competitors. For example, if you have an interview with Barclays bank what are its products, services and what makes it different from others like HSBC, NatWest. Find out what it is about the company that makes it appealing to you – does its values appeal to you most? If so what are these values and how? For example, working at Bloomberg appeals to me because 80% of its profits go to charity. Being someone who enjoys helping people and the community, this is quite appealing to me.

How do I Prepare Effectively for My Interview?

The final step is to identify skills, experience and knowledge required for the job as described in the person specification, then prepare yourself on how best to respond to these questions, which are mostly scenario based using the STAR approach.

How to Respond to Interview Questions Using the STAR Approach

The STAR method is a structured manner of responding to a behavioural-based interview question by discussing the specific situation, task, action, and result of the situation you are describing.

Situation: Describe the situation that you were in or the task that you needed to accomplish. You must describe a specific event or situation, not a generalized description of what you have done in the past. Be sure to give enough detail for the interviewer to understand. This situation can be from a previous job, from a volunteer experience, or any relevant event.

How do I Prepare Effectively for My Interview?

Task: What goal were you working toward?

Action: Describe the actions you took to address the situation with an appropriate amount of detail and keep the focus on YOU. What specific steps did you take and what was your particular contribution? Be careful that you don't describe what the team or group did when talking about a project, but what you actually did. Use the word "I," not "we" when describing actions.

Result: Describe the outcome of your actions and don't be shy about taking credit for your behaviour. What happened? How did the event end? What did you accomplish? What did you learn? Make sure your answer contains multiple positive results. Make sure that you follow all parts of the STAR method. Be as specific as possible at all times, without rambling or including too much information. Oftentimes students have to be prompted to include their results, so try to include that without being asked. Also, eliminate any examples that do not paint you in a positive light. However, keep in mind that some examples that have a negative result (such as "lost the game") can highlight your strengths in the face of adversity.

How do I Prepare Effectively for My Interview?

Sample STAR Response:

"Situation (S): Advertising revenue was falling off for my college newspaper, The Review, and large numbers of long-term advertisers were not renewing contracts. Task (T): My goal was to generate new ideas, materials and incentives that would result in at least a 15% increase in advertisers from the year before. Action (A): I designed a new promotional packet to go with the rate sheet and compared the benefits of The Review circulation with other ad media in the area. I also set up a special training session for the account executives with a School of Business Administration professor who discussed competitive selling strategies. Result (R): We signed contracts with 15 former advertisers for daily ads and five for special supplements. We increased our new advertisers by 20 per cent over the same period last year."

How do I Prepare Effectively for My Interview?

How to Prepare for a Behavioural Interview

• Recall recent situations that show favourable behaviours or actions, especially involving course work, work experience, leadership, teamwork, initiative, planning, and customer service.

• Prepare short descriptions of each situation; be ready to give details if asked.

• Be sure each story has a beginning, middle, and end, i.e., be ready to describe the situation, including the task at hand, your action, and the outcome or result.

• Be sure the outcome or result reflects positively on you (even if the result itself was not favourable).

• Be honest. Don't embellish or omit any part of the story. The interviewer will find out if your story is built on a weak foundation.

• Be specific. Don't generalize about several events; give a detailed accounting of one event.

• Vary your examples; don't take them all from just one area of your life.

Practice using the STAR Method on these common behavioural interviewing questions:

1. Describe a situation in which you were able to use persuasion to successfully convince someone to see things your way.

2. Describe a time when you were faced with a stressful situation that demonstrated your coping skills.

3. Give me a specific example of a time when you used good judgment and logic in solving a problem.

4. Give me an example of a time when you set a goal and were able to meet or achieve it.

5. Tell me about a time when you had to use your presentation skills to influence someone's opinion.

6. Give me a specific example of a time when you had to conform to a policy with which you did not agree.

7. Please discuss an important written document you were required to complete.

8. Tell me about a time when you had to go above and beyond the call of duty in order to get a job done.

9. Tell me about a time when you had too many things to do and you were required to prioritize your tasks.

10. Give me an example of a time when you had to make a split-second decision.

11. What is your typical way of dealing with conflict? Give me an example.

12. Tell me about a time you were able to successfully deal with another person even when that individual may not have personally liked you (or vice versa).

13. Tell me about a difficult decision you've made in the last year.

14. Give me an example of a time when something you tried to accomplish and failed.

15. Give me an example of when you showed initiative and took the lead.

16. Tell me about a recent situation in which you had to deal with a very upset customer or co-worker.

17. Give me an example of a time when you motivated others.

18. Tell me about a time when you delegated a project effectively.

19. Give me an example of a time when you used your fact-finding skills to solve a problem.

20. Tell me about a time when you missed an obvious solution to a problem.

21. Describe a time when you anticipated potential problems and developed preventive measures.

22. Tell me about a time when you were forced to make an unpopular decision.

23. Please tell me about a time you had to fire a friend.

24. Describe a time when you set your sights too high (or too low).

Why it is Important to Have a Mentor Whilst in Pursuit of Your Goal to Get an Apprenticeship or Job

A mentor is a "wise and trusted counsellor or teacher; an influential senior sponsor or supporter". The process of identifying, filtering, applying for suitable apprenticeships or job opportunities in line with your skills and passion is challenging, mentally, physically and emotionally draining. A mentor will help you to identify your strengths and weaknesses in terms of skills and knowledge and help you to identify your passion, if you do not know yours and ensure that you search for roles in line with your passion and strengths and support you to work on your weaknesses. They can develop a plan on how to achieve your goal of securing your apprenticeship of choice

Help you identify suitable roles, develop a CV, cover letter, apply for jobs and prepare you for interviews

Finally, he or she will be there to motivate and encourage you in challenging moments when you do not feel like carrying on e.g., after being unsuccessful in a few interviews

Then support you to identify why you were unsuccessful through regular review meetings, help you fill these gaps and achieve your ultimate goal of securing an apprenticeship of choice.

How do I Prepare Effectively for My Interview?

Are you in need of a career or apprenticeship mentor from A&F Tutors to support you in your journey to secure an apprenticeship of choice?

If so please contact us at: admin@aandftutors.com. You can also visit www.aandftutors.com for more information on our services and products related to 1-2-1 private tutoring, mentoring, apprenticeship and education consulting.

An apprenticeship could be the "golden ticket" to an individual's financial and career success, if the person takes, and uses the opportunity wisely.

What to do After Securing a Mentor and Making the Decision to Pursue an Apprenticeship

Begin your search and research for the right roles by exploring vacancies with companies that have been rated as the best places for apprenticeships.

How do I Prepare Effectively for My Interview?

According to The Job Crowd, find below the best 50 places for an apprenticeship covering different sectors. Click the link below please for more information:

https://www.thejobcrowd.com/companies/top-50-apprentice-employers/

Additional Resources

Get My First Job: www.getmyfirstjob.co.uk

A website with the aim of helping people looking to start their first job find an appropriate apprenticeship near them.

Rate My Apprenticeship: www.ratemyapprenticeship.co.uk

A website providing helpful information on reliable apprenticeships and a good place to research potential places to start working.

Not Going to Uni: https://www.notgoingtouni.co.uk/

A website aimed at finding apprenticeships and training opportunities for people who can't or don't wish to attend university.

How do I Prepare Effectively for My Interview?

The UK government link for apprenticeships: https://www.gov.uk/apply-apprenticeship

The UCAS link for apprenticeships: https://www.ucas.com/apprenticeships-in-the-uk

For those specifically interested in financial roles: https://investment2020.org.uk/

For those specifically interested in healthcare within the NHS roles: https://www.healthjobsuk.com

You can also search for apprenticeship roles directly on the NHS site: https://www.jobs.nhs.uk/

Printed in Great Britain
by Amazon